Where do you live?

أين تعيشين؟

ISBN: 979-8-9904050-7-3

Boston — New York — San Francisco — Baghdad
San Juan — Kyiv — Istanbul — Santiago, Chile
Beijing — Paris — London — Cairo — Madrid
Milan — Melbourne — Jerusalem — Darfur

11 Chestnut St.
Medford, MA 02155

arrowsmithpress@gmail.com
www.arrowsmithpress.com

The sixty-sixth Arrowsmith book was typeset & designed by
Gerard Robertson for Askold Melnyczuk & Alex Johnson in Garamond
Font

Where do you live?

أين تعيشين؟

a correspondence in Arabic and English
poems by Hanaa Ahmad Jabr
and Jennifer Jean

co-translated with Wadaq Qais
and Tamara Al-attiya

إلى الموصل..

الغربةُ
أن أرى اسمَك يبكي،
ولا أملكُ من الوطنِ ما يكفي
لمسح دموعهِ!
–هناء أحمد جبر

في كل غريبٍ،
لديّ صور كبيرة لِكُلُوِّي
عندما كانت بعمر هَيا. قافزة إلى الأبد...
–جنيفر جين

To Mosul...
Exile is to see your name weep,
And to possess from one's homeland so little,
To wipe away its tears!

-Hanaa Ahmad Jabr

In all my rooms, I've a large photo of Chloe
when she was Haya's age. She leaps forever...

-Jennifer Jean

CONTENTS

أين تعيشين؟

جنيفر جين

عليَّ أنْ أقولَ إنَّني أعيشُ في جسدي،
في المعرفة
وكان قدري - كما قلت يا هناء - في الشِّعر،
وحتَّى لو حاولتُ بجدِّية نفيه، "أقولُ كلَّ الحقيقة
لكنْ أقولُها منحنيةً* ." أحيا في هذه الأسرار
المكتوبة للفضوليين. أحيا في مدينة سالم
مع أشباحٍ متَّهمةٍ بالسِّحر. أعيشُ
في وادي سَان فرناندو في كاليفورنيا
في قصائدي. أعيشُ في الخوف
من الوحدة، لكنَّ موطني الحقيقي هو الغضب
كما يجبُ أنْ تكونَ الأمورُ بطريقةٍ
أفضل. قد قرَّرتُ الانتقالَ بعيدًا عن كلمة "يجب." أرغبُ في
القول إنَّني أعيشُ في سلام، إذا كنا نتحدَّثُ
عن انطواءِ الزَّمنِ إلى الآنَ، حيثُ يكونُ المستقبلُ الآن.

على الأقل أعيشُ في الحركة، على طول تلك الانحناءات
أحيانًا، عند حديثي معك يا هناء. عندما أحلِّقُ،
أعتقدُ أنَّني لطالما عشتُ في الهواء - من بوسطن إلى
كولكاتا - من سان فرانسيسكو إلى سيول. سألتُ طيارًا مرَّةً
عن موطنِ طفلٍ وُلد في منتصفِ الرِّحلةِ.
لم يكنْ يعرفُ مَاذا يجيبني. توقَّفَ
إلى الأبد. قد يقولُ
الحقيقةَ، ولكنَّها منحنيةٌ. لا أزالُ
أنتظرُ الأجوبة. كنت أعيشُ في الأيَّامِ الضَّائعة،
محدِّقةً بأشعة الشَّمسِ والأشجارِ. كَانتْ تضيعُ

15

عنّي حينها، ولكنْ ليس الآن. أعيشُ هناك الآن
في هذه القصيدة. يمكنك العيش إلى الأبد
في قصيدة. أعيشُ في منتصف التّكوينِ – عندما
أستطيعُ. إنّها أفضلُ طريقة للَحياة.

* اقتباس من قصيدة الشاعرة الأمريكية إميلي ديكنز تحت العنوان نفسه 1263.

Where do you live?

Jennifer Jean

I should say I live in my body,
in the knowledge
I was fated for—like you said, Hanna—poetry,
and—even if I try hard not to, I "tell all the truth
but tell it slant."* I live in these secrets
spelled out for the curious. I live in Salem
with the ghosts of accused witches. I live
in the San Fernando Valley in California
in my poems. I live in fear
of loneliness, but my real hometown is anger
at the way things are when they should be
better. I've decided to move away from should. I want to
say I live in peace, if we're talking
about time folding into the now, the future being now.

At least I live in motion, along those folds,
sometimes, when I'm talking to you, Hanaa. When I fly,

I think I've always lived in mid-air—from Boston to
Kolkata—from San Francisco to Seoul. I asked a pilot once
about the hometown of a baby born mid-flight.
He didn't know what to say. He paused
forever. He may have been telling
the truth, but slant. I'm still
waiting for answers. I used to live in wasted days,
staring at sunshine and trees. They were wasted
on me then, but not now. I live there now
in this poem. You can live forever
in a poem. I live in the middle of creation—when

I can. It's the best way to live.

*This is quoted from Emily Dickinson's poem number **1263**.

سيرتي الشّعرية

هناء أحمد جبر

سأخبرُك يا جنيفر عنّي،

كنتُ موجةً تائهةً ارتطمُ بكلِّ أغنيةٍ، ولا أعرفُ أيَّ طريقٍ إليَّ

لكنَّ الشّعر مدّ يديه!

رفعني،

عرّفني بي،

صيّرني طيراً يتجهُ نحو الجنوب،

الجنوبُ المسافرُ إلى حلم أبدي..

وجلسَ يقصُّ عليّ رحلةَ الاتجاهات:

الأطفالُ وبالوناتٌ ملوّنةٌ،

الوقت الذي يحرقُه الصّيفُ،

القبعاتُ الهاربةُ من عروض السّحرة،

الفراغُ الذي يتعثّرُ بنا،

الحقولُ التي نسيتْ مواعيدَ الحصادِ،

الجسورُ التي لا تؤدي إلى شيءٍ،

ومواسمُ توزيع الهدايا،

مقابل موتٍ، عفواً، مقابل صوتٍ أو نصفِ صوتٍ في الانتخاباتِ البرلمانية!

...

ثُمَّ يقسّم الرحلة بيننا:

لي سهراتُهُ..

أغنياتُه الحزينةُ..

صباحاتُ كلِّ نساءِ العالمِ..

دورانُ القصائدِ في البحثِ عنّي،

القصائدِ المبلَّلة بالحنين..

الرّسائلُ الأخيرةُ في كلِّ حربٍ!

كلُّ هذا لي، نعم لي

ولك أيُّها الشِّعرُ. . أنا

My Poetic Biography

Hanaa Ahmad Jabr

I will tell you my tale, Jennifer.

I was a lost wave crashing into every song.

But poetry extended his hands!

Raised me up,

introduced me to myself,

made of me a southward bird

migrating to an eternal dream,

narrating the journey, the route:

the children and vivid balloons,

the time that summer burns,

the shoddy fleeing from a magician's show,

the *horror vacui* stumbling upon us,

the field that forgot its date harvest,

the bridges going nowhere,

the gift-giving seasons

giving death, pardon, a voice…maybe, half-a-voice

in parliamentary elections!

...

Then, poetry divided the journey between us:

his late nights were mine…

his mournful songs…

and the mornings of all the world's women…

and the spun poems in search of me,

poems drenched in nostalgia…

the last message in every war!

All this is mine, yes—mine,

and for you, *O poetry*… I am.

العدو

جنيفر جين

"على جانبي، يتقلّبُ الشّيطان متلوّياً إلى الأبد"، بودلير في قصيدة الدمار.

عندما تقاتلَ الفَتَيان في المدرسة
تجمهر الفَتْيان
ومقاتلٌ ثالثٌ يتلوّى
حولهم ـ كالعادة ـ كأنّه
تينٌ أحمر. ابتعدتُ كأيّ شخصٍ مسالمٍ
وفي داخلي حرمتُ نفسي من دفء
المجموعة وحمايتها. متجرعةً خطر
المشي تجاه مقعدٍ هادئٍ،
فارغ. متجرعةً خطر
العَدم*. لكنّي يا هناء لمْ أردِ الجلوس
هناك. ولأنّي أعلم بذلك الآن. أرجوكِ
أنْ تجلسي معي يا هناء،
عندما يتقاتل الفَتْيان. للتّحدّث
عن حقائقَ أخرى
وعن بودلير، من الآن فصاعداً
عقلي بلغ الخريف!
أرمي فيه بذوراً
جَديدةً. ومن يعلمُ أيُّها ينجو؟**

* عبارة لاتينية ترجمت الى المعنى الحرفي للعربية، غالبا تسند الى صفات الفنانين.

** اقتباس من قصيدة الشاعر الفرنسي شارل بودلير عن قصيدته "Ennemi'L" أو ماتعرف
بـ "The Ruined Garden" بترجمة روبرت لويل.

The Enemy

Jennifer Jean

At my side the Demon writhes forever

        -Charles Baudelaire, in his poem "Destruction"

When two boys fought at school,
the kid crowd became
a third combatant—writhing
around the boys like a red
dragon—as usual. I
walked away like a good human—
when I was only
trying to abstain
from the warmth and protection
of a crowd, only trying out the danger
of a walk towards a quiet,
empty bench. A *horror
vacui.* But—I didn't want to sit,
Hanaa. I know that now. Please,
sit with me, Hanaa—

when two boys fight. Let's talk
of other facts
and Baudelaire, **From now on,
my mind is autumn!
...I throw fresh seeds
out. Who knows what survives?

*A latin phrase meaning "a fear of the void" which usually refers to artists.

**These are lines from "L'Ennemi" also known as "The Ruined Garden" by
Charles Baudelaire, translated by Robert Lowell.

ريدٌ غيرُ سريٍّ للغاية

هناء أحمد جبر

لا وطنَ أدسُّ رأسي في صدرِه وأبكي،

لا حربَ تقتلُ ذاكرتي

(هكذا أجيبُ عيني " جنيفر" وهما تنصتان لسيرةٍ أصابعي)

لا يدَ تلوّحُ من فوق الجسرِ العتيقِ!

لا جارَ يراعي حاجتَنا لصوتِ فيروز..

لا حقيبةَ أحفظُ فيها فساتين سهرٍ وصورةً لشفتيّ قبل اليباس!

لا حبيبَ يهاتفُني صباحًا هامسًا:

استيقظي.. ليصحو العالمُ،

لا أهلَ يصلحونَ للهجرانِ لأزجَّ نفسي في أقربِ منفى..

لا صديقَ يربّتُ على كتفِ حزني

ويجعلُ يدي تتوقفُ عن التّلويحِ لموتٍ قريبٍ

فالموتُ هو أنْ نتوقّعَ حدوثَهُ!

Very Non-Classified Information

Hanaa Ahmad Jabr

No homeland keeps a chest where my head can cry.

No war kills my memory.

(That's how I answer your eyes, Jennifer, which listen to my hand's life story.)

No hand waves over the old bridge!

No neighbor takes into account our need for the voice of Fairuz.

No luggage keeps my evening dresses—and a picture of my lips before they dry!

No lover calls me in the morning, whispering, *Wake up, let the world wake up…*

No family is fit for my leaving—for plunging myself into the nearest exile.

No friend strokes the shoulder of my sadness

nor stops my hand which welcomes Death.

Death is to expect Death!

حربٌ أُسيطرُ عليها

جنيفر جين

مثل الجميع عارضتْ أُمّي الحربَ،

أحبتِ الحربَ

المتجسّدةَ في جُنديٍّ،

في أبي. وفي أحد الأيّام عند الغسق، عانقتهُ وسألتهُ

عن ... "الحربِ؟". لاحقاً

عندما اجتاحَها الخوفُ، أخبرتهُ أنْ يختبئ

في المنزلِ إلى الأبد- فدفعَها من شقّتهم المطلّةِ على الشّاطئ

وقفلَ البابَ عليها. لكمتِ البابَ بكفّيها

طوال الغسق لمطلع اليوم التّالي. أتذكّرُ هذا.

ربّما استمعتُ من منزلي ململمةً ذاتي

إلى مصدرِ كلِّ الأرواحِ. أو ربّما رحمها. أو من

قبو غير محصّنٍ في داخل شقّةٍ مظلمة

في مهدي نصف المحترق. تخيّلتُ في بادئ الأمرِ

انفجاراً كبيراً، وربّما كان صدى طرقاتها الأخيرةِ

متردّداً عند الفجر، ومدى استيعابِها للحرب

بحجم بقعةِ حبر

في هذه الكلمةِ وفي هذا السّطرِ وفي هذه القصيدةِ وفي هذا الكتابِ،

بحجم مكتبةٍ عالميةٍ لحربٍ يعرفها.

الخلاصة، إنّني أثرٌ لنهايةِ حربٍ صغيرةٍ اندلعتْ

بين رجلٍ وامرأة

فكنتُ الذّرةَ الوحيدةَ لحربٍ أُسيطرُ عليها.

The War I Control

Jennifer Jean

Like everyone, my mother protested war,

made love to the war

possessing the body of my soldier

father. She held him close, one dusk, and asked

about "… The war?" And later—

when fright gripped her, said, *Hide at home*

forever—he shoved her from their beach-side apartment

and locked the door. She banged fists on the door

all dusk and into the following day. I remember this. Maybe

I listened from my real home—snuggled up

to the source of all souls. Or, from her womb. Or, from

an undefended bunker—inside that dark

apartment, in my half-burnt crib. I imagine,

in the beginning was the big bang. And maybe her last,

echoing bang at dawn meant: her grasp of war

was as vast as a droplet of ink

in the word, in the line, in the poem, in the book,

in the universe-sized library of the war he knew.

Meant: I'm the tail-end of a small war

between a man and a woman—

which is the only iota of war I control.

إلى الحرب كالعادة

هناء أحمد جبر

كامرأةِ الثّلجِ (يوكاي)*
تخرجين أمامه
مرّة تتظاهرين بالتّعبِ ...
يسندُك
فيتعثّرُ طريقَهُ إلى القصيدةِ،

ومرّة أخرى
تقصّين له خرافةَ جمالكِ
والطريقَ الذي دخّن كلَّ أمنياتِك
تقفين بين يديه
بين عينيه
بين رئتيه
الحلمُ يقتربُ... يبتعدُ
الحلمُ يبتعدُ.. يقتربُ
الكلماتُ تتلاشى كلّما اقتربتِ
وحين يسطعُ ضوءٌ مفاجئٍ.... تجاهَه
تذوبين.

*امرأة الثلج أو يوكاي هي من الأساطير اليابانية القديمة لشبح امرأة يتجول في الثلج.

To War, as Usual

Hanaa Ahmad Jabr

Like the Yuki-onna*
you emerge before a man
pretend fatigue…
And, he aids you
stumbles on his way to the poem
And, once again
you show him the myth of your beauty
and the road that smoked all your hopes
You stand
between his hands
between his eyes
between his lungs
The dream approaches... it retreats
The dream retreats... it approaches
Words fade as you draw near
and when a sudden, stark light shines...

you melt away

*Yuki-onna or the Snow Woman is an old Japanese myth of a woman's ghost
wandering in the snow.*

قراءة الروايات في أربعينات عمري

جنيفر جين

عندما أقتربُ من ذلك المحيط،

أتذكّرُ رغوةَ الماءِ الكثيفةَ وهي تلتفُ

حول عظامي المسنّة. تلك- بشرتي

الشّابةُ. أخترقُ

الأمواجَ بابتسامةٍ مضطربة.

أمّا الآن- فأنا

لا أسمح أبداً لأيِّ أصبعٍ في قدميّ بأنْ يتبلّلَ.

عندما تعلو شيئاً فشيئاً

ضوضاءُ تلك الأفعوانية

فوق رؤوسنا، حتى تحطَّ

بسرعةٍ إلى الأرضِ،

أسمعُ صرخةً

رائعةً- كصرخة صف رابع تقليدية.

وهي

نهايةُ

تلك القصّة. عندما أذهبُ إلى النّومِ

لا أستطيع أنْ أنامَ ولا أستطيعُ

استحضارَ تلك الرّاحة.

32

أنا متأكّدةٌ بأنّني اعتدتُ

الانعطاف-بسرعةٍ- لكن-ليس نحو الأحلام

بل نحو الغموضِ اللذيذِ. بطريقةٍ ما،

أتنفّسُ الآن،

وبسرعةٍ هائلةٍ لأقعَ عميقاً

في الحبِّ مرّةً أُخرى.

Reading Fiction in My 40's

Jennifer Jean

When approaching that ocean,
I recall thick foam flowering
around my old
bones. That is—my young
skin. Breaching
breakers with an unfixed
smile. Now—I never
let a toe get wet. When
that roller coaster
clacks by degrees
overhead, bolts
fast to earth, I hear a fabulous
shriek—a fourth grade standard.
Which is
the end
of that story. When I go to sleep
I do not go to sleep—and, can't
recall that rest.
I'm certain I used to
drift—promptly—into—not dreams—
but sweet mystery. Somehow,
I breathe, now, too
fast to fall that deep
into love again.

رصيف الكتب*

هناء أحمد جبر

الأرصفةُ الصدئةُ**
تشتاقُ الكتبَ
وتطالبُ الشّوارعَ الفارغةَ
بوقفِ إطلاقِ الحزنِ
على المارة،
وكنسٍ تسكعِهم!

* رصيف الكتب تأسس بعد دمار الشارع الثقافي في الموصل، العراق 2018. مكان لتجمع كل المهتمين بالكتب بمختلف أنواعها.

** كتبت هذه القصيدة في 2021، أثناء كوفيد-*19*

Sidewalk of Books*

Hanaa Ahmad Jabr

The rust rotten sidewalk**
longs for strewn books,
asks hollowed streets
to: *Ceasefire sorrow*
piercing pedestrians—

sweep up their aimlessness!

Sidewalk of Books was established after the destruction of the cultural street in Mosul, Iraq 2018. A place of gathering for all those interested in books of all genres.

**This poem was written in 2021 during COVID-19.*

الصقارون

جنيفر جين

لا أعرفُك يا هناء حتى الآن، ولا أعرفُ هل سبق وإنْ سمعتِ عن

مدينة تنسل. وهل سبق أن أسرَكِ قصرُ

السّرد ذلك، أو البائع المتجوّل

ذلك الذي يبيعُ حكايا الأبطال- رغم أنّها حبكةٌ "مبرمجة لنا".

نحن خلّاقون باحتمالية

نطاردُ الخاتمة. نبدأ معاً،

نمشي غرباً نحو جادةِ الغروب،

بعيداً عن متحفِ صناعة الموت، نحو

مدرسة هوليوود. نقف قليلاً تحت مظلّة متّسخة

في فندق باجت إن، المكان الأخير

الذي احتجزني فيه والدي، والدي الذي اتعبتُه الحربُ. كان الأمرُ غريباً جداً. احتجزني

مرّة أخرى، سابقاً، قبل ثمانٍ وأربعين سنة.

مضى على الأمر عام فأر لعام فأر آخر.

انحنتِ السّماء الكوبالتية علينا

مثل كلّ مرّة. هذه المرّة، كان هنالك بابٌ نحو مركز إعادة تأهيل

ظل يقرع مفتوحاً. بعدها،

سمحتُ له بالذّهاب للمنزل

لغرفة الفندق. استدرتُ غرباً. لنتسابق نحو الغرب

معاً، يا هناء، وليغدو المشهد سعيداً–

37

ك ''صورة صغيرة من روح العالم'' .

فوقنا، نجوم كثيرة نحاسية وباهتة، تتبعثر على شارع الكرمة

حيث يتجوّل السياح.

لكن إنسانيين معاً، بدلاً من ذلك– لنتفوق على شمس الغروب.

يجب أن نكون كاليفورنيين. سنحتاج سيارة مكشوفة–

على الرغم من مقتي لهذه الأمور: فالسماء وسمومها المحتملة

تدخل دائما. يدخل الاحتراق اللامع.

إن كنتِ تودّينَ قيادة السيارة، قوديها.

تفوّقي على ضوء الخريف

بيد على الباب، ويد على العجلة.

التفي حول رياح سانتا آنا الدافئة.

أشيري نحو كل نخلة مزروعة، كل طائر عاسوق حط.

أركني في نهاية الجادة،

في شاطئ غلادستون. ومعاً، في الموقف هذا،

سنشاهد سحاب حلوى شعر البنات، والتوهج الأرجواني

فوق حركة المحيط البارد. بكلماتنا،

سنحوّل كلّ صقور المينا الزائفة إلى هدية،

إلى الحرية في هواء نقي.

سنعيد كتابة هذه المدينة،

نحقّق قصص المحبة في الشّاشة الفضية. *

* هذه السطور مقتبسة من أغنية فندق كاليفورنيا لفرقة إيغلز، قصيدة ''القدوم
الثاني'' بقلم W.B. Yeats وفيلم الصقر المالطي.

38

The Falconers

Jennifer Jean

I don't know you, yet, Hanaa. I don't know if you've heard of
Tinsel Town. If you'd ever be drawn to this Palace
of Narrative, this Hero's Journey
peddler—though, this plot is "programmed
to receive" our kind. We are potential
creators. We chase denouement. We'd begin together,
walk west on Sunset Boulevard,
away from the Industry of Death Museum, towards
Hollywood High. Pause under a grimy awning
at the Budget Inn—the final place
my war-torn father held me. It was so odd. He'd held me
once before, forty-eight years before.
It'd been one *Year of the Rat* to another *Year of the Rat*.
The cobalt sky slouched against us
each time. This time, the door to a drug rehab center
kept slamming open. Then,
I let him go home
to his motel room. I turned west. Let's race west
together, Hanaa, and let that scene be happy—
a small "image out of *Spiritus Mundi.*"

Above us, so many dull brass stars litter Vine

Street, where all tourists trek.

Let's be human together, instead—outstrip the setting sun.

We'll need to be Californian. We'll need a convertible—

though I hate those things: the sky and its potential

poisons always enter. A glittering burn enters. And

if you want to drive, drive.

Outpace the autumn light

with one arm on the door, with one hand on the wheel.

Wind around the warm Santa Ana winds.

Point out every transplanted palm, every perched kestrel.

Pull in at the end of the Boulevard,

at Gladstone's Beach. And together, in this lot,

we'll face the cotton-candy cumulous, the periwinkle glow

over cold ocean motions. With our words,

we'll remake every fake enamel falcon into a gift,

into freedom in clean air.

We'll rewrite this town, make true all

silver screen sisterhoods, all

"the stuff that dreams are made of."*

*With lines from the song "Hotel California" by the Eagles, the poem "The Second Coming" by W.B .Yeats, and the movie The Maltese Falcon.

ثلاث حكايات

هناء أحمد جبر

-أحدّثُكَ عن الأرضِ التي
تبلعُ أحلامَ الحبيباتِ والأمهاتِ، وحلوى العيد ..
الأرضُ التي تبلعُ الجنودَ وتحوّلُهم إلى سواتر،
ومدنٍ جديدةٍ،
ونصبٍ مجهولٍ،
وذكرياتٍ طاعنةٍ في الوجعِ!

..

أحدّثُك عن الليالي التي
أصبحتْ فيها كلُّ القصائدِ مريبةً
والزّوايا بلا سكينةٍ،
والضّوءُ جرحٌ تنزُّ منه شهقاتٌ لا حدودَ لها.

..

أحدّثُك عن
كلِّ حربٍ وثّقتْ تاريخَها بثقبٍ في صوتي
حتى أصبحَ ناياً..

Three Tales

Hanaa Ahmad Jabr

I talk to you, the other, about a nation
consuming the dreams of lovers, mothers,
          and the holiday sweets of Eid.
About the soil swallowing soldiers—
          turning them to mounds,
new metropolises,
faceless monuments,
and recollections that are obedient
          to stabbing pain.

I talk to you, the other, about nightfalls
turning the poems suspicious,
the corners restless,
and the light into a wound from which boundless
          gasps ooze.

I talk to you, the other,
about the way each war documented its history
          with a hole in my voice
until it became a flute.

ثلاث حكايات

جنيفر جين

تحاولُ أُمِّي أنْ تُقنعَني

أنَّها لَمْ ترحلْ عنّي

لسبع سنوات. أقودُ عبر شوارع مدينةِ سالم.

هذهِ لعبةٌ خطرةٌ. لكي أفوزَ،

يجبُ أنْ لا ألعب. يجبُ أنْ لا أودَّ اللّعبَ.

يمكنني فقط السّيطرة على المركبة. تنفّسي.. اغفري

أكثر وأكثر- هذا يعني تسليطَ الضّوءِ على

الحقيقةِ- مع ذلك،

وكما تقولين يا هناء، «الضّوءُ يُصبح جرحاً

تنزُّ منه شهقاتٌ لا حدودَ لها»

جزءٌ من حكايتي الثانية

الحكايةُ التي لَمّ تسرديها لي يا هناء. هي أنّني ولدتُ

في الرابع من شهر يوليو. نحن نرقصُ

حول هذه الحقيقةِ، ونحن بالرّقصِ

تعرّفنَا على بعضِنا البعض.

43

الحكايةُ الثالثة هي أنني أريدُ السّيطرة أيضاً

بينما الإله مسيطرٌ.

هناء، إذا مشينا في شوارع مدينة سالم، وتبادلنا أطرافَ الحديثِ، وشعرنا بريح
دافئة،

لم نطلبْ من ذلك النّسيم بأنْ يلامسَ

شَعرَنا. وذلك يذكّرني

بالوقت الذي أخبرتني به التكنولوجيا بأنّ كلمةَ شَعر باللغة العربية

هي ذاتُها كلمة شِعر- وهو لغزٌ جميلٌ. *

Three Tales

Jennifer Jean

My mom tries to convince me
she didn't leave me
for seven years. I'm driving through Salem.
This is a dangerous game. To win,
I can't play. I can't want to play.
I can only grip the wheel. Breathe. Practice
forgiveness—which means shining a light—on
facts—even though,
as you say, Hanaa, *light becomes a wound*
from which boundless gasps ooze.

A part of my second tale is
the tale you didn't tell me, Hanaa. I was born
on the fourth of July. We dance
around this fact, but dancing is how
we know each other.

The third tale is that I want control
when God is in control.
Hanaa, if we walk Salem's streets, talk, and feel
a warm wind,
we did not tell that breeze to touch our
hair. Which reminds me
of the time technology told me the Arabic

word for hair
is the Arabic word
for poetry—which is a lovely mystery.*

*The words "Poetry" and "Hair" share a similar root in Arabic.

التلاشي.. آخر أخباري

هناء أحمد جبر

ظننتُ أنّني غفوتُ-يا صديقتي- بعد آخر رسالةٍ منه،
لكنَّ هناك صوتاً غريباً
أشبه بكرةٍ زجاجيةٍ سقطتْ ببطءٍ،
صوتٌ لا يتوقّفُ،
لا توقفهُ الشّظايا التي تناثرتْ
ولا تلفّهُ لحظةُ صمتٍ.. كما يحدثُ بعد كلِّ دحرجةٍ..
أنظرُ عبر النّافذةِ.. لا شيءَ.. كلُّ شيءٍ هامدٍ،
سياجُ البيت
والأشجارُ.. وبضعُ نجماتٍ في رداءِ اللّيل..
لكنّ الصّوتَ مستمرٌّ..
أقفزُ من فراشي،
أنزلُ السّلالمَ.. لكنّ الصّوتَ يلاحقني..
تذكرتُ حينها
أنّ الأصواتَ التي خارج البيت لم تعدْ تخيفني
ولا التي داخله أيضاً..
لكنّ هناك شيئاً يرافقني
لملمتُني... ثمّة كرةٌ من دمي
لا تزالُ تتدحرجُ.. في داخلي
أشعرُ أنّها تتكمشُ
شيئاً
فشيئاً..
تتكمشُ بفعلِ رسالته الباردةِ!

47

The Dissolution...My Latest News

Hanaa Ahmad Jabr

I thought I'd dozed—my friend—after his last message.
But there was an odd sound
like a ball of glass falling, slowly,
like something unbroken,
unbroken by the crash of shards scattering
or by the usual moment of silence after a globe rolls away.
I looked out the window...at the nothing, at the everything lifeless.
At fencing.
At unmoved trees…and, some stars robed by night…
Still, that noise persisted…
So, I jumped from bed,
descended the stairs...and the disturbance stalked me…
I remembered, then,
that hullabaloo outside the house no longer frightens me,
that hullabaloo inside the house no longer frightens me.
Still—I have a stalker.
And I have to hug myself… feel my blood clotting,
rolling... inside me.
Feel a recoil,
a little by little…
a shrinking because of his icy message!

السّنةُ القمريّةُ*

جنيفر جين

هنالكَ انعكاسُ وجهٍ في الإناءِ النّحاسي، قرب بحيرةِ الضّفدع القديم** .

باقترابي يتّضحُ أنّهُ ليسَ وجهي،

ليسَ تماماً. مجرد مساحةٍ زرقاء أو تدفقاتٍ بلونين اثنين، البنفسج والبرتقالي

أو حركة الغيوم- كما لو أنّ نسمةَ هواءٍ

داعبتْ خصلاتِ شعرِ امرأةٍ بدأ الشيب يجتاحه. لو تسمّرتُ فوقه،

فوقه تماماً،

فوق ذلك الإناء، لعكسَ ملامحي المتموّجةَ،

تشدُّ الجاذبيةُ كلا خدّيّ الممتلئين وجفني عينيّ المرتخيين،

أرى العدو والحبيبَ،

يرونني مؤطرةً بصغارِ التّماثيلِ البرونزيةِ، الممحوةِ،

جالسين طوال حافةِ ذلك الإناء. طيور الكاردينال،

ونقار الخشب والحسّون، يحلقون عالياً وواطئاً

قرب تلك الأراضي المغلقة والقريبة

هناك حيث ستبدأُ سنةُ التّينِ الأزرقِ الجديدةُ. الجميعُ

يقولُ أنّها ستكونُ سنةً غريبةً، سنةً فظيعةً.

وحتى أصوات آخر ليالي كلِّ يوم، الأصواتُ الغريبةُ،

تلك التي تشبّهُها هناء أحمد جبر، بكرةٍ زجاجيةٍ

49

سقطتُ ببطءٍ، متوقّعةً الخوفَ وتباعاته،

أهم مخطئون؟ في هذه اللحظة،

أنا الجميعُ– وهذا أشبهُ بقولي إنّني واحدةٍ بين عديد

من التّماثيلِ الممحوةِ، جالسةً على حافةٍ

إناءِ العالم. وجهي متسمّرٌ

لا يعتريني الخوفُ ولا أتوقّعُ

تفاحاتٍ حمراء وخضراء وبيضاء

وملوّنةٌ. كراتُ الحلوى ببطءٍ تسقطُ

وبطعم الهشاشةِ الأخيرةِ

قبل سنةٍ جديدةٍ، قرب بحيرةِ الضّفدعِ القديمِ،

حيثُ أكونُ

متوسّطةَ اللامكان– بيقينٍ ثابتٍ

الرّبيعُ خلفي،

الرّبيعُ أمامي.

*السنة القمرية أو سنة لونار وهي تنسب إلى الحضارة الصينية في تتبع مراحل اكتمال القمر عند تسجيل التاريخ. كتبت هذه القصيدة في 2024 مجارية لبداية السنة القمرية للتنين الخشب. هذه القصيدة عن عمل فني بصري لمنحوتة في البحيرة، بعنوان ''أجلس فقط'' لـ لندا هوفمان.

**بحيرة الضفدع القديم هي مزرعة تقع في هارفارد، ماساتشوستس.

Lunar New Year*

Jennifer Jean

There's a face in the big bronze bowl near Old Frog Pond.**
It's not my face, exactly,
as I approach. Only an azure expanse, or
a layering of violet and tangerine streams,
or a cloud movement—as if a breeze
lifted the locks of a silvering brunette. If I hover above, exactly
above, the bowl, my wavering features
warp the water,
gravity pulls on my new jowls, on loose skin above my eyelids.
I see the enemy and the beloved
sees me framed by the small, smudged, and still bronze figures
seated along the edge of that big bowl. Cardinals,
Flickers, and Finches alight and aspire
in the nearby orchard—
where, soon, the blue dragon new year will bloom. Everyone
says it will be a crazy, a terrible year.
Even the odd sounds that tear at
the middle of every night—
the ones Hanaa Ahmad Jabr likens to *a ball of glass, slowly
falling*—anticipate fear and its fruit.
Are they wrong? Right now,
I'm everyone—that is to say: one among many
smudged figures on the edge
of the bowl of the world. My face is so still,

I unknow fear and do not anticipate

the Blushing, the Greening, the Golden, the Nonesuch

apples. The balls of sweet, slowly

falling. The taste of the last of the crisp

before another new year near Old Frog Pond, where I can be

grounded in the midst of some unknowing—knowing

Spring is behind me,

Spring is before me.

*Lunar New Year or Moon Year, is linked to the Chinese culture in tracking the phases of the moon in recording dates. This poem was written in 2024 aligning with the start of the Year of Wood Dragon. This is an ekphrastic poem based on a sculpture at the Pond, titled "Just Sitting" by Linda Hoffman.

**The Old Frog Pond is a farm in Harvard, Massachusetts.

فتاة الحي (إلى جنيفر جين)

هناء أحمد جبر

"لم تكنْ تشعرُ بالوحدة،

فوحدتُها معها "-كما يقولُ ذلك شاعرٌ عراقي-*

وهذا الحيُّ المريبُ

لم يكنْ سوى لغزٍ لا يهمُّها فكَّه!

تجاهلتْ صمتَه المفاجئ،

بيوتَه المتشابكةَ،

أبوابَهُ الصّغيرة،

وجدرانَه الدّاكنة

التي تشبهُ أغصانَ شجرةِ لوزٍ وحيدةٍ..

...

فتاةٌ لا يهمُّها سوى السّماءِ التي تستلقي فوق بيتِها،

وسورِ بيتِها الذي يمنعُها من رؤيةِ العاطلين عن الحياةِ،

فتاةٌ لا يهمُّها سوى تلك السّماءِ..

التي تراها عند الفرحِ

بحراً يتموّجُ بهدوءٍ....

53

وعند النّعاسِ

خرافاً صغيرةً تركضُ باتجاه الأفقِ..

وعند الحزنِ... شيئاً مِنْ كحلِ أمِّها

..

وعند كلِّ عودةٍ من المدرسةِ

تقفزُ عبر عتبةِ بابِ بيتِها برجلٍ واحدةٍ،

وهي ترمي وراءَ ظهرِها حزمةَ لأشياءَ لا تهمُّها..

وهكذا استمرَّ شريطُ حياتِها...

دخلتُ ذلك الحيِّ طفلةً..

.

.

.

وخرجتُ شاعرةً!

*اقتباس تمت إعادة صياغته عن الشاعر عدنان الصائغ.

A Girl of the Neighborhood (for Jennifer Jean)

Hanaa Ahmad Jabr

"She didn't feel lonely,/ For her loneliness was with her"

-Adnan Al-Sayegh

And this eerie neighborhood
was a mystery she didn't care to solve!
She ignored its sudden silences,
twined apartments,
narrowed doors,
shadowed walls
like the branches of a lonely almond tree…
A girl cares only about the azure ocean above her home
and every border keeping her from the lifeless ones.

…

A girl cares only about that sky.
When joyful
this girl saw serenity in the waves of that sea…
When drowsy
she saw little lambs galloping at that horizon...

When mournful…she lined her eyes with her mother's kohl…

With every return from school—
with one foot, she'd leap over the doorstep,
deserting a hefty bundle of things, she hated…
And so, the movie of her life carried on…
She'd crossed the threshold: a child.

.

.

.

She'd leave—later—a poet!

ظهيرة مشتعلة*

جنيفر جين

وهل أخبرتُك يا هناء

أنّ التّاريخَ الأمريكي مؤطرٌ بالسّينما؟ نحن

نشاهدُ مبارزَيْنا يتقابلان

عندما تكونُ الشّمسُ في وسط السّماء

عندما يكونُ تبادلُ إطلاقِ النّارِ عادلاً

عندما لا يعاني أيٌّ منهما من عائقٍ

سوى الكراهيةِ

وقصرِ النّظرِ وجحودِ النّعمةِ والغرورِ.

يؤمنُ بعضُنا بهذا المشهدِ.

يؤمنُ بعضُنا ببكاءِ نسائِهم المغبرات

في البيوتِ. ولكنْ–

يؤمنُ بعضُنا بحقيقةِ

السّماءِ الزّرقاءِ الصّافيةِ

حيثُ يمكنُ لجسدينِ التّألق بأشعةِ شمسِها،

نرى ذلك جنوبَ المركز

لطريقٍ ترابيٍّ في بلدةٍ ريفية

نرى ذلك لمسافاتٍ طويلة بتفحّصِ سمات

وجوهِ بعضهم البعض ومعانيها. معجزةٌ! نظنُّ

أنّ غيابَ الظّلّ هو جنةٌ.

وهي جنةٌ فقط

إنْ لمْ يكنْ لدينا ما نخفيه. دعينا نلتقي هنا يا هناء،

على الطّريق الرّئيس لهذهِ المدينةِ المشتركةِ

مع مترجمتِنا وَدَق. وبمجردِ

أنْ نعتادَ على سوءِ

الفهم التّام المزعجِ ما بيننا،

سنعرفُ الجنّةَ، سنعرفُ

أنّ الصّداقةَ ممكنةٌ.

*ظهيرة مشتعلة هو عنوان فيلم من أفلام الغرب الأمريكي 1952.

High Noon*

Jennifer Jean

And did I tell you, Hanaa,
American history is wrapped in film? We
watch our gunslingers meet
when the sun is directly overhead
so the gunfight is fair,
so neither man is blinded by anything
other than hatred,
shortsightedness, ingratitude, ego.
Some of us believe in this scene.
Some of us believe in their dusty women
crying at home. But—
some of us believe in the fact
of a clear sky so blue
two bodies can: bathe in sunlight,

see down the center
of a dirt road in a rustic hometown,
see for miles, see into the niches and nooks of
each other's faces. A miracle! We

think this lack of shadow is heaven.
And it's only heaven
if we've nothing to hide. Let's meet
here, Hanaa,
on the original road of this mutual hometown
with our translator, Wadaq. And once
we all get used to the terrible
discomfort of imperfect understanding,
we'll know heaven, we'll
know friendship is possible.

High Noon is the title of an American western movie made in 1952.

بورتريه

هناء أحمد جبر

لا مفرَّ من هذ الحزن..

لا مفرَّ من ذراعيه وهما تزجّاننا في أقربِ حربٍ،

لا مفرَّ من أصابعه،

وهي تشكّلُنا ككرات ثلجٍ في منطقةِ شرقيةٍ..

سرعان ما نتلاشى..

ولا من شراهتِه

وهو يلوكُنا كوجبةٍ طازجةٍ..

لا مفرَّ من أفكارِه المتلاطمةِ

وهو يدخّنُ أحلامَنا ببرود ... ذهاباً وإياباً.

ها هو السّاحرُ.. كالعادة

يقتربُ..

يقتربُ.. إنّه هنا!

يصنعُ قبعةً له من رؤوسنا..

وقفّازَين من جلودِنا..

وينتعلُ ما تبقى من حياتِنا..

ثُمَّ يعلنُ نصرَهُ وهو يقفُ على خردةٍ.. هي أشلاؤنا..

نصرٌ على ماذا؟

لا أعرفُ!

ربّما

نصرُّ على بقعةِ ضوءٍ بعيدةٍ في أعماقِنا!

..

يا اللّه لقد سُرقَ منا حتى حزننا..

كيف نحزنُ بعد الآن؟!

Portrait

Hanaa Ahmad Jabr

There's no running from our sorrow...
from his grip, as he drags us into the nearest war.
No running from his fingers,
molding us like snowballs from an Eastern region...
though, we vanish—fast...
No running from his mean greed
as he devours us all like new food...
No running from his rattling ideas
as, cold and cool, he smokes our dreams... going and coming.

He's coming close, this necromancer... as usual.

Closer...
Closer... and, here !
He crafts his *chapeaux* from our skulls...
gloves from our skin...
he wears the remains of our lives...
declares his win while standing on our carnage...
But a win over what?

I don't know!
Maybe
our distant spark of light!

(Oh God, he's stolen even our sorrow...
Now how do we grieve?!)

عن قصيدتك (بورتريه)

جنيفر جين

إجاباتٌ يتمُّ اعتبارُها:

باعتذاراتٍ مبهمةٍ ومطوّلةٍ لمواساتي

أو إلى حكومتي، تفاصيل كوابيس دستوبيا

مليئة بمعادن صدئة وحادة

وصراخ مستمر، بخوفٍ

من شتاءٍ نوويٍّ نرتمي تحت المكتبِ

بذاكرةِ طفلٍ في الصّفِ السّابعِ

بتقاريرَ إخباريةٍ عن شظايا، قديمة منها وجديدة

صمتٌ، أملٌ، قصصٌ

تحكي عن امرأةٍ ابتلعَها ثعبانٌ البورمي

أرادتِ الاطمئنانَ على خنازير

حقلِ ذرتِها، فوجدَها الثّعبانُ،

لدغَها، وسحقَها، وابتلعَها.

ثمَّ- كتبَ ثلاثةُ شعراءٍ أصدقاء،

سونيتات ببطولةِ هذه المرأة، وهذا الثّعبان.

دعَوني لمشاركتِهم الكتابةَ، فكتبتُ ''كيف

تقتلُ الثعابين؟'' أكثرتُ فيه بالنّظريات، وكره الأفاعي

لمحلول الفم الأزرق، ولهيب ولاعة البك،

وبتر منجل لمكان أسفل الذقن، وكيف أننا لا نستطيع

حبَّهم للموت. وبكلِّ حال، الحربُ

تأكلُ الحُبَّ، فيغدو الحبُّ كتلةً دهنيةً بمعدةِ وحش.

تركضُ العائلةُ والأصدقاءُ بعيداً، مذعورين ومنتحبين ليجدوا

أثرَ قدمٍ ما، وفردةَ خفٍّ ومشعلاً، ثُمَّ

بعد قطعِهم لتلك الحراشفِ، قرب موضع الانتفاخ

وجدوا تلك المرأةَ ميتةً.. بزي تجوالٍ بسيطٍ. يا هناء، لقد شاهدتُها

مكشوفةً، شاهدتُها من خلف أصابعِ يدي.

هذا كلُّ ما أستطيعُ فعلَهُ

قراءةَ قصائدِك، كتابةَ قصائدِي، والحياةَ ما بينهما.

Regarding Your Poem "Portrait"

Jennifer Jean

Possible responses include:
vague extended apologies for my comfort
or my government, details of dystopian nightmares
complete with sharp rusted metal
and unbroken screams, below-the-desk nuclear-winter
fears from seventh grade, half remembered
news reports of shrapnel—both ancient and recent—
silence, hope, stories
about a woman swallowed by a Burmese python.
She wanted to check on the pigs
in her cornfield. But he found her,
bit her, crushed her, consumed her.
Then—three poet friends wrote sonnets
starring this woman, this python.

They invited me to write one too, so I wrote: "How
to Kill Pythons!" It was full of theory, and snake hatred
of blue mouthwash, lit Bic lighters,
machete chops below the jaw line. And how
you certainly can't love them
to death. Anyways war
eats love. Love's a fat lump in the belly of a beast.
Family and friends run out, search, wail—find
a footprint, a slipper, a torch, and then—

after slicing through scales, near the bulge—
a broken woman, dressed for a stroll. Hanaa, I saw her
unveiled—my eyes squinting between my fingers.
And this is what I can do. Read
your poems. Write my poems. Live between the two.

الغرفة المجاورة

هناء أحمد جبر

سأحكي لك يا جنيفر،

عن غرفةٍ مجاورةٍ،

لمْ أعرفْ شكلَها الدّاخلي ربّما تكونُ كبيرةً كقارّةٍ،

أو صغيرةً كحقيبةٍ مدرسيةٍ،

أو ملتويةً كأغصانِ شجرةِ العنبِ،

أو رحيمةً كقلبِ أمٍّ!

أو ربّما تكونُ عميقةً كبئرٍ..

أو مظلمةً كبطنِ حوتٍ، نعم،

لمْ أرَها، لمْ أرَ شيئاً، لمْ تكنْ عيناي معي

حتّى قلبي كان يقفزُ باكياً بين وجوهِ الأطباءِ،

باحثاً عن لحظةِ أمانٍ لجسدِ صديقتي،

رُلى* كذلك لمْ ترَ شيئاً، سوى حوتٍ!!

حوتٌ لا لونَ لهُ،

وهو يبتلعُها شيئاً فشيئاً! ويتركُ يديها ملوّحتين للحياةِ،

بينما كانتْ كرياتُ دمِها تتدحْرجُ في كلِّ اتجاهٍ،

شعرتُ حينها أنّني بحاجةٍ إلى الانزواءِ في أقربِ قصيدةٍ،

قصيدةٍ تُربّتُ على كتفي،

وتسحبُ يدَيْ صديقتي من حزنِها الأخيرِ،

قصيدةٍ ترى كلّ «كانيولا» في جسدِها .. زهرةَ «لوتس»،

وكلَّ صرخةٍ تُطلقُها .. كلمةَ «لا»،

وكلَّ دمعةٍ تعانقُ وجهَها .. كلمةً من اللّه!

...

رأيتُني أتخبّطُ في رأسي،

من يدري قدْ أكونُ بحاجةٍ إلى نظريةٍ علمية –حقاً– تؤكّدُ لي أنّ الحياةَ كذبةٌ!

لا يُهمني بعد أنْ يكونَ أعذبُ الشّعر أكذبَهُ–كما يقال–

أحتاجُ قصيدةً صادقةً حتى وإنْ كانتْ مُرّةً، قصيدةً كحياتِنا التي توشكُ أنْ تفلتَ منّا في كلّ حربٍ، فتعيدُها إلينا «الصّدفةُ»!

ها أنا أجلسُ في الأرضِ،

وأسندُ رأسي إلى حائطِ العناية المشدّدةِ،

وأنا لا أزالُ أمتلكُ من الدّموع والدّعاءِ ما يكفي؛

لأقنعَني بأنّ صديقتي لا تزالُ آمنةً في غرفةِ العملياتِ المجاورةِ،

وأنّها سترسمُ لي –بعد قليل– شكلَ تلك الغرفة!

*تجمع رلى وهناء أحمد جبر صداقة وثيقة دامت لـ 20 عاما.

The Next Room

Hanaa Ahmad Jabr

I will tell you, Jennifer,
about the next room.
I did not know it might be a continent—
or as small as a school bag,
or as twisted as the branches of a grapevine,
or as merciful as a mother's heart,
or maybe deep like a well,
or dark like the belly of a whale.
      Yes—
I didn't see it. I did not see a thing.
My eyes were not with me,
even my heart wept agony
between the faces of each doctor,
wept for solace for my friend's body,
for Rula,* who only sees the whale!
A whale of no color,
swallowing her slowly, except two shaky hands,
her blood cells slipping in every direction,
and me escaping to the nearest poem,

to a poem stroking my arm,

pulling my Rula's hand from her latest tragedy,

transforming every cannula needle into a lotus,

and every scream into a "NO!"

and every slipping tear into God's word!

...

I saw myself stumbling,

craving a scientific theory literally confirming life is a lie!

Not caring if the purest poetry is a lie—as they say—

needing an honest, bitter poem, like life on the verge of every war,
    returned to us by "coincidence!"

Now, I'm on the ground,

resting my head against the wall of her ICU

with enough tears, prayers

convincing me Rula is safe in the OR, Rula will soon paint me that
    room shape!

*Rula and Hanaa Ahmad Jabr have been close friends for 20 years.

أين تعيشُ الفتياتُ الصغيرات

جنيفر جين

في كلِّ غرفةٍ، لدي صورٌ كبيرةٌ لكلُووِّي*

عندما كانتْ بعمرِ هَيا**. قافزةً إلى الأبدِ

من منتصفِ كومةِ أوراقِ أكتوبر

في مدينةِ سالم. أوراقٌ ذهبية،

برونزية ووردية وحمراء، تلك الأوراق

تقفزُ أيضاً. كلُّ ورقةٍ منها ساكنة، وضبابية من الحركة.

بقميصِها المخطط أفقيا بالأبيض والأسود،

بهذا المشهدِ. بنقاطٍ بيض متناثرةٍ على بنطالِها الأسود

تحلِّقُ عائمةً في الهواءِ بحذاءٍ زهريٍّ

على تزاحمِ أوراقِ الخريفِ الجميلةِ

وأوراقِ الأشجارِ على الأرضِ هادئةً. فاتحةً ذراعيها

نحو الأبدِ، بابتسامةٍ كبيرةٍ مثل ابتسامة

هَيا عند ارتدائِها لزي التّخرّجِ لأوّلِ مرّةٍ

أتتذكرين هذه

الفرحةَ؟ أنا أتذكّرُها وأحملُها معي

يومياً، متأملةً قفزتَها في مواسمَ أخرى.

*كلوي هي ابنة جنيفر جين

*هيا هي ابنة أخ هناء أحمد جبر

Where Little Girls Live

Jennifer Jean

In all my rooms, I've a large photo of Chloe*
when she was Haya's** age. She leaps forever

from the center of a pile of October
leaves in Salem. Gold,

bronze, blush, rust. The leaves
leap too. Every one is still, smudged, in motion.

Horizontal white and black stripes cut across her shirt,
the scene. White dots scatter down her black pants.

Two candy pink shoes hover
above the messy joy of autumn

foliage on the chilling earth. Her arms are as wide as
forever, her smile as wide as

Haya's when she wore her first cap and gown.

Do you remember this
delight? I do, and carry it
daily, gaze at its leaping in the off-season.

*Chloe is Jennifer Jean's daughter.

**Haya is Hanna Ahmad Jabr's niece.

شجرة المشمش*

هناء أحمد جبر

لم أشعرْ بوحدتي يوماً،

طالما أستظلُّ تحت شجرةِ المشمش،

أخطُّ على جذعِها بعضاً من أمنياتي،

وعنوانَ كتابي الشِّعري الجديد

فتخضّرُ من شدّةِ الفرح!

-يبدأ المشهد:

(في كلِّ صباح

تبدو الشَّجرةُ متشابكةً مع أشعة الشمس

كأنّهما يتسابقان في رسم أكثر من ظلٍّ فوقي،

بينما تقفُ على أغصانِها عصافير كثيرة،

عصافير ترتدي أزهارَ الشَّجرة،

تبدو كأنّها فريق فتياتٍ مستعداتٍ للرّقص بقيادة الجميلة كلووِّي**

ها هي تطرقُ الغصن بقدميها الناعمتين

فتنثرُ الأزهار في كلِّ مكان... وتتبعُها طرقاتُ أقدام الفتيات...!

هكذا سيكونُ المشهد حالما لو كنتُ في دولة أخرى

وكنتُ أنا مدربةَ رقص..

لكنّني بكّاءةٌ ومن العراق!)

77

-يبدأ المشهدُ مرّةً أخرى

في الحقيقة لم يكن هناك صباحٌ حقاً

لم أرَ الشّجرةَ.. لثلاثِ سنواتِ حربٍ متتالية

حربٌ لم تعطِنا أيّةَ فرصةٍ للقاء!

وعوّدتْنا على الوداع!

حربٌ تسمح لنا أنْ نبكي كما ينبغي..

لم أرَ الشّجرةَ.. لم أستطعْ حينها، كنتُ أخشى أنَ تصلني رصاصةُ قنّاصٍ لا يحبُّ
فكرةَ الحياة!

كنتُ أفكرُ

هل أجرؤ على البكاء أمامَها،

ربُما حزني كبير عليها!

كنّا متشابهتين

لم نرَ الليلَ في الليلِ،

ربّما كنّا هاربتينِ من بعضنا

هـي تمدُّ جذورها عميقاً في كلِّ أجزاءِ حديقة بيتنا

وأنا أستلقي بين أكثر من جدارٍ

أفكرُ في شكلِ السّماءِ.. وهلْ لونُها أزرق كما هو!

وفي لونِ الشّجرةِ.. ربّما يكونُ أخضرَ حقا!

- المشهدُ في مرّاتٍ أخرى

هل أخبرتُك يا وَدق، أنّ الشّعرَ نبوءة؟

حسنا.. سأخبرُك،

في إحدى ليالي الحرب

لم نكنْ وحدنا وسط الرصاص والقنابل،

تبا إذا كانتِ الحربُ لعبةً

فشجرةُ المشمش حارسُ مرمى محترف،

لقد وقفتْ شامخةً.. لتصدَّ عنّا أكثر من شظية!

لقد تناثرتْ أشلاؤها في كلِّ أجزاء حديقتنا الكبيرة!

تحطمتِ الشّجرةُ لتحمينا.. لم تفكرْ في ذلك،

لأنّها أمٌّ، الأمُّ تفعلُ ولا تفكر!

ارتجلتِ المشهدَ كلَّه،

هي شجرةٌ متحطّمةٌ... وأنا شاعرةٌ بكّاءة!

شجرةٌ لم تنحنِ..

نعم،

سابقا كتبتُ في قصيدةٍ لي:

"للأشجارِ مبادئ

لا تنحني لأزيز الإنذار!" ***

نعم الشّعر نبوءة.

*شجرة المشمش هي شجرة حقيقية في الفناء الخلفي لمنزل هناء أحمد جبر تعرضت لقصف عشوائي 2016، وتصدت له حامية المنزل وعائلة هناء من الدمار التام.

**تخرجت كلوي، ابنة جنفر جين، من مدرسة الرقص أثناء كتابة هذه القصيدة.

*** من المجموعة الشعرية «أجرُّ حزني من ياقته» لهناء أحمد جبر

The Apricot Tree*

Hanaa Ahmad Jabr

I'm never lonely
beneath the apricot tree,
carving some of my wishes into her trunk,
carving the title of my new poetry book
as she blossoms with joy!

-The scene starts like this:
[Every morning
the tree entangles a ray of sunlight
as if racing to cast more shade
as flocks perch on her limbs,
as birds clothe themselves with her flowers,
as if they're a flock of dancers led by beautiful Chloe**
tapping the branches with her soft feet
scattering petals...followed by all the girls tiptoeing...!
And this is the dreamy scene, if I were in another country
if I were a dance instructor...
But I'm just a weeper from Iraq!]

-The scene starts again:
In truth, there was no morning.
I didn't see the tree... over three years of constant war
kept us from meeting!

We were affable with goodbye!

We were allowed to weep, as we should…

But I didn't, couldn't see her… when dreading snipers detesting
  life!

Anyways, I was thinking,

Do I let her see me weep?

Maybe my sadness is oversized!

We were similar.

We did not see night at night.

Maybe we ran from each other,

her roots sinking deep into every part of our garden,

and me lying between more than one wall,

pondering the look of the sky… whether it's a true blue!

Pondering the color of the tree… maybe it's a true green!

-The scene at other times:

Did I tell you, oh Wadaq, that poetry is prophecy?

Well, let me tell you—

on one war night

we were not alone with bullets and bombs.

And, damnit, if war is a game

then the apricot tree was a pro goalkeeper,

standing tall… shielding us from splintered shrapnel!

Her limbs scattered over our wide garden!

She shattered for us… without thinking,

because a mother protects without thinking!

And she improvised that scene

between her broken tree-ness... and my weeping poet-ness!

She did not bend...

So yes,

I wrote once, in my own poem:

"Trees have principles,

they do not bow to the roar of alarm!"***

So yes, poetry is prophecy.

*The Apricot Tree is an actual tree in the backyard of Hanna Ahmad Jabr's house that happened to stand against a random bombarding in 2016, sheltering the house and Hanaa's family from a complete destruction.

**Chloe, Jennifer Jean's daughter, graduated from a dancing school during the writing of this poem.

***From the poetry collection of Hanaa Ahmad Jabr, "I Draw My Sorrow From His Collar."

نطرونا كتير*

جنيفر جين

الموسيقا أصعبُ من الأخبارِ، فهي تبعدنا

من أراضي الحربِ إلى الأفلامِ

تفصلُنا، وتجبرُنا..

في بداية حياتنا غطّينا صمتَ أفلامنا

بـــبيانو أجدادِنا، وفي النّهايةِ

كشفَها النّغمُ السّري

فهطلتِ الدّموعُ،

أينما وجدتَّ أرضُ الحربِ في قلوب النّاسِ. وهي في وجدانِهم

لطبيعةٍ بشرية. وإنّي لأعتقد يا هناء

أنّ حادثَ سيّارةِ أختِك ولاء** جنوب الموصل، لهُ إيقاعٌ

في تذكره، تلك الهيوندا الصّفراء في حفرةٍ على جانب الطّريقِ

أربعةُ أطفالٍ في ذهولٍ وذعرٍ في المقعد الخلفي. الكلُّ بأمانٍ

وربّما على أنغام فيروز،

نطرونا كتير! نطرونا نطرونا، آه.. نطرونا...

المعنى، الصّبر، الموسيقا هي لفتةٌ

إنسانيّةٌ أكثر من تاريخيةٍ. كأغلبِ العائلاتِ أو كلحظةٍ.

لحظةُ الصّمتِ التي أسمعُ بها

83

وتر النّغمةِ السّريّةِ

أتكون البدايةُ... لنهايةٍ أثيرةٍ؟ أم مجرد رصاصةٍ طائشةٍ أخرى..

في نزاعٍ أهوج على أرضٍ ما. وفي مثل هذه اللحظةِ

أقدّمُ رفضي للألعابِ الجماعيّةِ، فالابتعادُ عنها هو قاعدتي.

لستُ مثاليةً لأيِّ شخصٍ

وهي كلمةٌ صعبةٌ. أضعفُ من الحُبِّ،

أبعدُ من الكرهِ. ومثل الحبِّ الموسيقا لا تُترجمُ بمثاليةٍ

يا هناء، إنّ الموسيقا تجمعُنا معاً، في مركبةٍ ذهبيةٍ

مثل العائلة.

*نطرونا كتير: أغنية مشهورة للمغنية العربية فيروز.

** ولاء هي أخت هناء أحمد جبر، كتبت هذه القصيدة بعد تعرضها لحادث سير مع عائلتها.

84

Natarouna Keteer*

Jennifer Jean

Music is harder than news. Shoves news
from a front into a movie.
It cleaves us. It is compulsion:
in the beginning, we blanketed the silence of our pictures
with tin pan piano; in the end, *the secret chord*
will tear out tears
whenever there's a front in the heart.
And there always is—
given human nature. I'm guessing, Hanaa,
your sister Walaa's car crash in Southern Mosul has a track
in memoriam. The yellow Hyundai in a ditch,
four children startled in the back seat. Everyone safe:
to a tune by Fairuz, maybe —*Natarouna Keteer!*
Natarouna, natarouna, aaaahhhhh…natarouna…

Meaning, patience. Music is a gesture
more human than historical. Like most families. Or, a minute
of silence. The moment I learn
the secret chord—strike it—

could be the beginning

of an important end. Or, just another stray bullet

in a stray feud on a front. Like the moment

I say, *I don't play team sports.* The caveat being: "as a rule"

since I'm not anyone's perfect.

Which is a hard word. Weaker than

love, further than hate. And like love, music is perfectly un-

translatable—

it gathers us together, Hanaa, into a golden vehicle

like family.

*Natarouna Keteer is a song by the Arabic singer Fairoz; the direct translation of the title is "They waited for us, a lot."

الحياة مركبة صفراء

هناء أحمد جبر

لم تكنِ الموسيقا وحدها ضمن سيرتي الذاتية،
بل رافقتْها الحربُ،
فكلُّ أغنيةٍ تشيرُ إلى موتي ﰲ إحدى الحروب،
نعم يا صديقتي،
الموسيقا التي لا تزالُ تجمعُنا،
علّمتْنا أنّ الحياةَ تسيرُ بشكلٍ متعرّجٍ،
بشكل طولي، أو عرضي
المهمُ أنّها لا تتّخذُ مساراً مستقيماً كالضّوءِ،
ولا صوتاً إيقاعياً عذباً،
ترانا الحياةُ أرقاماً صحيحةً،
تدهسُنا دفعةً واحدةً،
لا يهمُّها ذعرَ الأطفالِ،
دعاءَ الأمهاتِ،
كعكةَ عيدِ الميلاد،
وأكثرَ من أغنيةٍ لفيروز...
تدهسُنا الحياةُ...فنتسلّلُ من تحت قدميها،
فنخرجُ صفراً على جهة الشِمال
إنّها تقتاتُ علينا،
ومنذ أوّلِ مشوارٍ لنا فيها
أكّدتْ لنا أنّها ليستْ سوى
مركبةٍ صفراءٍ!

87

Life Is a Yellow Vehicle

Hanaa Ahmad Jabr

Music alone wasn't part of my biography,

it was a companion of war.

And, every song refers to my death in some war.

Yes, my friend,

music is compulsion—it brings us together,

teaches us that Life prefers to wind

up, down, across.

Life doesn't follow a straight path like light

or a sweet rhythmic sound.

She sees us as integers.

Tramples us, all at once,

despite a child's panic,

a mother's prayer,

a birthday cake,

a song by Fairuz...

She stomps us... so we sneak from under her feet,

emerge as Zeros on the left side.

She feeds on us,

confirms to us that she is nothing but

a yellow vehicle.

الحصان في حركته

جنيفر جين

تاريخي هو تاريخ الأفلام.
ولدنا في كالفورنيا وترعرعنا معاً. لكن
سُمي أول فيلم بـ الحصان في حركته*. وعندما حاولتْ تلك الكاميرات القديمةُ
تصويرَ فرسٍ عربيٍ رائع-
فرسٌ بريةٌ متمردةٌ تجري على مقربة من ممر مونتغمري
رفعتْ كلَّ حوافرها عن الأرض أيضاً.

معجزة! يا هناء، أهمستُ لك
أنَّ أمي أحرقتْ كلَّ قصائدها في برميل؟ أأخبرتُك
أنَّ أمّي كانتْ من رعاة البقر؟ كانتْ تمتطي حصانَها بلو
إلى وسط ساحةِ رعاةِ البقرِ الصّاخبة
وترمي الحبالَ ممسكةً بالعجولِ الصغيرةِ للفوزِ بالمال. لا،
أنا لا أمتطي الخيولَ. ولكنْ نعم،
أشاهدُ أفلامَ الغربِ الأمريكي. أريدُ أنْ أفهمَ الرّجالَ

والنَساءَ والخيولَ
والأفلامَ. آلاتُ السّرد البارعة! مثل القصائد-
أنتِ وأنا وأمّي، نريدُ أنْ نكونَ "سطراً

مشدوداً لدرجة أنّهُ يغنّي"، كما كتب فيليب مترس**. نأمل
أنْ تكونَ محادثاتُنا– حتى الكلمات المحترقة لأمّي
مثل لقطاتٍ ثابتةٍ من ذلك الفيلم الأول. معجزات منتصف الهواء
تواقةٌ إلى أرضٍ صلبةٍ.

The Horse in Motion

Jennifer Jean

My history is film history. We
were both born and bred in California. But
the first film was named *The Horse
in Motion.* * And, when those ancient cameras tried
to capture a beautiful racing Arabian—
one wild Mustang in nearby Montgomery Pass
lifted all her feet off the ground, too.

A miracle! Hanaa, did I whisper,
my mom burnt all her poems in a barrel? Did I tell you
my mom was a cowgirl? She'd ride her stallion, Blue,
to the center of a rowdy rodeo arena
and rope fast calves for prize money. No,
I don't ride horses. But, yes,
I do watch Westerns. I want to understand men

and women and horses and
film. Powerful narrative machines! Like poems—
you and me and my mom, want to be: *a line*

so taut it sings, as Philip Metres** wrote. We hope
our conversations—even mom's words of ash—
are like stills from that first film. Mid-air miracles
akin to solid ground.

*Referring to the first documented movie in 1878 which recorded the
movement of a horse using pictures.*

**From Philip Metres' poem "We Are All God's Poems"*

أين تعيشين؟

هناء أحمد جبر

لا أذكر اسم أول حرب ولدتني
ربما لم يدونها أحد،
ربما يعرف ذلك نهر دجلة،
وحده من يعرف الاتجاهات،
وحده من يحفظ الخرافات والحقائق
التي رافقت جريانه منذ القدم،
أعيش هناك في الشمال حيث كل ذكرى قابلة للوجع،
أنتمي إلى النهر،
ها أنا عند إحدى ضفتيه، أقف بعين مفتوحة،
وأراقب حطام المدينة القديمة وهو يندثر..
وأهمس «يا رب الأزقة القديمة.. احفظنا من الحرب القادمة»!
ها أنا أراقب:
«باب شمس»* وهو يعود إلى الحياة
سور نينوى
تمثال أبي تمّام** وهو يلوّح للقادمين،
الجسور وهي تربط رئتي المدينة،
الغيمات وهي مستعدة للمطر بوضوح دون دخان يحجبها،
تدفق النهر دون جثث حرب توقفه!
وكثير من الأرصفة...
وأشياء أخرى لا تتسع نشرات الأخبار لذكرها، ولا برامج التنمية البشرية،
ولا حتى تقارير الـ BBC أو CNN بكل قنواتها..!
..
نعم أعيش هناك..
بينما تحاول عيني الثانية وهي مغمضة أن تخبئ أكثر من مشهد عن بشاعة
الحرب..
لا شيء يساعدني على وصف ذلك،
لا حكايات الجدّات،

ولا أحلام الأطفال!

لا مهرجانات الشعر، ولا كتب النقد، ولا أفلام الرعب!

لا تقارير الأمم المتحدة، ولا أي كتاب يؤرخ لذلك،

لا جملة بأية لغة كانت تقوى على حمل تلك البشاعة!

ها أنا أشعر بتوّرم عيني من ذلك كله،

أرشيف عليّ حمله للأجيال القادمة،

ها هو وجهي ينتفخ كذلك

ذراعاي

جسدي

ياه.. ها أنا أتكور.. أعاود الانتفاخ من جديد

وأرتفع.. أظنني سقطت نحو الأعلى، كالعادة.

الآن، ربما تتساءلين يا جنيفر:

- من أنت؟ ما مدينتك الأم؟

وسأجيب فوراً وإحدى عينيّ لا تزال مغمضة: -

- نحن هاتان العينان معا.. وإلى الأبد.

**باب شمس، إحدى البوابات الأثرية في مدينة نينوى (مدينة الموصل الحالية، العراق) رمّم بعد
تحرير الموصل عام 2017.

**تمثال أبي تمام هو تمثال شاعر عربي معروف أعيد بناؤه بعد الدمار الذي تعرض له من قبل
قوات داعش (التي احتلت الموصل من 2014-2017)، يعد التمثال من المعالم السياحية للموصل
في العراق.

Where do you live?

Hanaa Ahmad Jabr

I don't know the name of the first war that birthed me.

Perhaps no one recorded it.

Perhaps the Tigris witnessed it,

alone knowing every direction,

alone remembering the myths and the facts

attending its flow since forever.

I live here, in the North, where memory is bloody sorefull,

where I belong to the river

and stand on one bank, one eye open

staring at the ruins of the old city, decaying...

whispering, *Oh God of old alleys... protect us from the next war!*

Here I am, watching

the Shamsh Gate* reanimating,

the walls of Nineveh,

the statue of Abu Tammam* waving to arrivals,

the bridges connecting the lungs of the city,

the clouds eager for rain, unobscured by smoke,

the river rushing without bodies of war to stop it,

   and many more sidewalks...

And other things breaking news can't mention, nor rehab for
  PTSD,

nor reports from the BBC or CNN, nor any channels!

..

Yes, I live here...

While my other eye is closed, hiding dreadful war scenes…

With nothing to help me form a description,

not grandmother's tales,

nor children's dreams!

Not poetry festivals, nor literary criticism, nor horror movies!

Not UN reports, nor history texts.

No sentence in any language could bear the weight of that terror!

Here, I feel my eyes swelling with it all,

carrying The Archives for future generations.

And here my face swells, too.

My arms.

My torso.

Oh…I'm here, embracing myself… swelled again

and rising… I think I fell upwards, as usual.

Now, Jennifer—you may wonder:

"Who are you? What is your hometown?"

And I'll answer immediately—with one eye still closed.

We are the two eyes together… forever.

*Shamsh Gate, one of the ancient gates in the city of Nineveh (currently the city of Mosul, Iraq) it was restored after the liberation of Mosul in 2017.

**The statue of Abu Tammam is a statue of a well-known Arab poet that was rebuilt after the destruction it was subjected to by ISIS forces (which occupied Mosul from 2014-2017). The statue is one of the tourist attractions of Mosul in Iraq.

NOTES

Hanaa Ahmad Jabr's dedication was written in March 2016 in Mosul.

Jennifer Jean's dedication was written in July 2024 in Salem and is from her poem "Where Little Girls Live."

ACKNOWLEDGEMENTS

Many thanks to Iraqi artist Jenan Mohamad for producing the cover art.

Many thanks to Miled Faiza for copy-editing the Arabic text.

Many thanks to Francesca Bell at the *Los Angeles Review,* to Jose Araguz at *Salamander Magazine,* to the team at *The Common,* and the team at the *Arrowsmith Journal* for publishing many of these pieces online in both Arabic and English.

Many thanks for funding—and encouragement—go to: the women of the Her Story Is collective—especially Amy Merril; the Fort Point Theatre Channel; the Essex County Community Foundation's Creative County Initiative; the Iraqi and American Reconciliation Project; the Golden Thread Theater; the Center for Arabic Culture in Boston; and the team at Arrowsmith Press—especially Askold Melnyczuk, for believing in this project.

BIOGRAPHIES

Dr. Hanaa Ahmad Jabr was born in Mosul, Iraq. She is a prize-winning poet and short story writer who has participated in critical conferences and international poetry festivals. She has a PhD of Philosophy in Arabic Literature. Her books include the poetry collections *I Draw My Sorrow from His Collar*, and two books of criticism: *The Dialectic of Poetry* and *Prose in Modernist Poetry*, and *The Poetics of the Prose Poem*. Additionally, she's released a children's book: *Sultan and Shanidar*. Hanaa teaches at the University of Mosul.

هناء أحمد جبر ، شاعرة، ناقدة، ومدربة في الكتابة الإبداعية، أستاذة جامعية. ولدت في مدينة الموصل في العراق، حاصلة على دكتوراه فلسفة في الأدب العربي، تكتب في مجال الشعر والنقد وأدب الطفل، حاصلة على جوائز في الإبداع الأدبي، لديها مشاركات في مؤتمرات نقدية ومهرجانات شعرية عالمية، من مؤلفاتها:

في الشعر: أجرُّ حزني من ياقته، وكتابان في النقد: جدلية الشعر والنثر في شعر الحداثة، وقصيدة القطاع الخاص «شعرية قصيدة النثر».

وكتاب قصصي في أدب الطفل: السلطان وشانيدار. هناء تدرس في جامعة الموصل.

Jennifer Jean was born in Venice, California in America. She is the author of *VOZ, The Fool, Object Lesson*, and *Object Lesson: A Guide to Writing Poetry*. She's the editor of *Other Paths for Shahrazad :A Bilingual Anthology of Contemporary Poetry by Arab Women* (Tupelo Press, 2026). She's received honors from DISQUIET, the Kenyon Review Writers Workshop, the Mass Cultural Council, and the Academy of American Poets. Her poems and co-translations have appeared in *Poetry, Rattle, On the Seawall, the Los Angeles Review, The Common*, and elsewhere. Jennifer is an organizer for the Her Story Is collective, a core faculty member at the Solstice MFA program ,and the senior program manager of 24 PearlStreet–the Fine Arts Work Center's online writing program.

جنيفر جين ولدت في فينيسيا، كاليفورنيا في الولايات المتحدة الأمريكية. هي مؤلفة كتب "VOZ"، "المجنون"، "درس الشيء"، و "درس الشيء: دليل على كتابة الشعر". وهي محررة لكتاب "طرق أخرى لشهرزاد: مختارات شعرية ثنائية اللغة للنساء العربيات المعاصرات" (توبيلو بريس، 2026). حصلت على تكريمات من DISQUIET، ورشة عمل مجلة كينيون، المجلس الثقافي لولاية ماساتشوستس، وأكاديمية الشعراء الأمريكية. تظهر قصائدها وترجماتها المشتركة في مجلة POETRY، وRattle، وOn the Seawall، ومراجعة لوس أنجلوس، و The Common ومواقع أخرى. جنيفر هي المنظمة في مجموعة Her Story Is، وهي عضو هيئة تدريس أساسي في برنامج Solstice MFA، ومديرة برنامج 24PearlStreet – برنامج الكتابة عبر الإنترنت في Fine Arts Work Center

Tamara Al-attiya is a freelance writer and translator; she teaches translation at Almaaqal University in Basra, Iraq. Tamara is the founder of the Qantara Foundation of Culture, Heritage, and Arts.

تمارا العطية كاتبة ومترجمة مستقلة؛ تدرس الترجمة في جامعة المعقل في البصرة، العراق. كما انها المؤسسة لمؤسسة القنطرة للثقافة والتراث والفنون.

Wadaq Qais was born in Basra, Iraq. She received a degree in accounting in 2021. Later, she found her true calling in the Translation Department at the University of Basra, College of the Arts, where she is completing her studies. Reading provided her a gateway to other worlds, allowing her to broaden her perspective and expertise in the disciplines of both literary and business translation.

ولدت ودق قيس في البصرة، العراق. حصلت على البكالوريوس في المحاسبة في عام 2021 ثم وجدت ميدانها الحقيقي في قسم الترجمة في جامعة البصرة، كلية الآداب، حيث تكمل دراستها. قدمت لها القراءة بوابة لعوالم أخرى، مما سمح لها بتوسيع وجهة نظرها وخبرتها في تخصصات الترجمة الأدبية والترجمة التجارية.

Books by

ARROWSMITH

PRESS

Girls by Oksana Zabuzhko

Bula Matari/Smasher of Rocks by Tom Sleigh

This Carrying Life by Maureen McLane

Cries of Animals Dying by Lawrence Ferlinghetti

Animals in Wartime by Matiop Wal

Divided Mind by George Scialabba

The Jinn by Amira El-Zein

Bergstein
edited by Askold Melnyczuk

Arrow Breaking Apart by Jason Shinder

Beyond Alchemy by Daniel Berrigan

Conscience, Consequence: Reflections on Father Daniel Berrigan
edited by Askold Melnyczuk

Ric's Progress by Donald Hall

Return To The Sea by Etnairis Rivera

The Kingdom of His Will by Catherine Parnell

Eight Notes from the Blue Angel by Marjana Savka

Fifty-Two by Melissa Green

Music In—And On—The Air by Lloyd Schwartz

Magpiety by Melissa Green

Reality Hunger by William Pierce

Soundings: On The Poetry of Melissa Green
edited by Sumita Chakraborty

The Corny Toys by Thomas Sayers Ellis

Black Ops by Martin Edmunds

Museum of Silence by Romeo Oriogun

City of Water by Mitch Manning

Passeggiate by Judith Baumel

Persephone Blues by Oksana Lutsyshyna

The Uncollected Delmore Schwartz
edited by Ben Mazer

The Light Outside by George Kovach

The Blood of San Gennaro by Scott Harney
edited by Megan Marshall

No Sign by Peter Balakian

Firebird by Kythe Heller

The Selected Poems of Oksana Zabuzhko
edited by Askold Melnyczuk

The Age of Waiting by Douglas J. Penick

Manimal Woe by Fanny Howe

Crank Shaped Notes by Thomas Sayers Ellis

The Land of Mild Light by Rafael Cadenas
edited by Nidia Hernández

The Silence of Your Name: The Afterlife of a Suicide
by Alexandra Marshall

Flame in a Stable by Martin Edmunds

Mrs. Schmetterling by Robin Davidson

This Costly Season by John Okrent

Thorny by Judith Baumel

The Invisible Borders of Time: Five Female Latin American Poets
edited by Nidia Hernández

Some of You Will Know by David Rivard

The Forbidden Door: The Selected Poetry of Lasse Söderberg
tr. by Lars Gustaf Andersson & Carolyn Forché

Unrevolutionary Times by Houman Harouni

Between Fury & Peace: The Many Arts of Derek Walcott
edited by Askold Melnyczuk

The Burning World by Sherod Santos

Today is a Different War: Poetry of Lyudmyla Khersonska
tr. by Olga Livshin, Andrew Janco, Maya Chhabra, & Lev
Fridman

Salvage by Richard Kearney

In the Hour of War: Poetry From Ukraine
edited by Carolyn Forché and Ilya Kaminsky

A Crash Course in Molotov Cocktails: Poetry of Halyna Kruk
tr. by Amelia Glaser and Yuliya Ilchuk

Don't Close Your Eyes by Hanna Melnyczuk

Tiny Extravaganzas by Diane Mehta

Departures from Rilke by Steven Cramer

On the Road to Lviv by Christopher Merrill
tr. into Ukrainian by Nina Murray

Nothing Bad Has Ever Happened
A Bouquet to Victoria Amelina

The Farewell Light by Nidia Hernández

Downfall of the Straight Line by Charles O. Hartman

The God of Freedom by Yulia Musakovska
tr. Olena Jennings and the author

Away Away by Mark Pawlak

The Miró Worm and the Mysteries of Writing by Sven Birkerts

St. Matthew Passion by Gjertrud Schnackenberg

New and Selected Poems by Glyn Maxwell

A Precise Chaos by Jo-Ann Mort

Coming Ashore by Thomas O'Grady

ARROWSMITH is named after the late William Arrowsmith, a renowned classics scholar, literary and film critic. General editor of thirty-three volumes of *The Greek Tragedy in New Translations*, he was also a brilliant translator of Eugenio Montale, Cesare Pavese, and others. Arrowsmith, who taught for years in Boston University's University Professors Program, championed not only the classics and the finest in contemporary literature, he was also passionate about the importance of recognizing the translator's role in bringing the original work to life in a new language.

Like the arrowsmith who turns his arrows straight and true,
a wise person makes his character straight and true.

— Buddha

www.ingramcontent.com/pod-product-compliance
Lightning Source LLC
Chambersburg PA
CBHW020754130626
46554CB00006B/2178